THE MATT MERTON
MYSTERIES

CHANGING SIDES

Paul Blum

RISING ★ STARS

nasen

NASEN House, 4/5 Amber Business Village, Amber Close,
Amington, Tamworth, Staffordshire B77 4RP

Rising Stars UK Ltd.
22 Grafton Street, London W1S 4EX
www.risingstars-uk.com

Text © Rising Stars UK Ltd.
The right of Paul Blum to be identified as the author of this work has
been asserted by him in accordance with the Copyright, Design and
Patents Act, 1988.

Published 2010

Cover design: pentacor**big**
Illustrator: Chris King, Illustration Ltd
Photos: Alamy
Text design and typesetting: pentacor**big**/**Clive Sutherland**
Publisher: Gill Budgell
Editorial consultants: Lorraine Petersen and Dee Reid

British Library Cataloguing in Publication Data.
A CIP record for this book is available from the British Library.

ISBN: 978-1-84680-798-5

Printed by Craft Print International Limited, Singapore

THE MATT MERTON
MYSTERIES

CONTENTS

THE CRASH

The Crash happened in 2021. Alien spaceships crash-landed on Earth. Now the aliens rule the world. They have changed shape so they look like people. People call the aliens The Enemy. Since The Crash, people are afraid. They don't know who is an Enemy and who is a friend.

An organisation called The Firm keeps order on the streets. The Firm keeps people safe from Enemy attacks – or do they?

People are going missing and the Earth is becoming colder and darker all the time. A new ice age is coming ...

5

ABOUT MATT MERTON

Matt Merton works for The Firm. He often works with **Dexter**. Their job is to find and kill The Enemy. They use Truth Sticks to do this.

But Matt has problems. He has lost some of his memory and cannot answer some big questions.

Where has **Jane**, his girlfriend, gone?

How did he get his job with **The Firm**?

Matt thinks The Firm is on the side of good. But he is not sure ...

CHAPTER 1

Two men walked into Sam's cafe. They worked for The Firm. They were their most deadly agents. They were not smiling.

'Turn off the music,' said the tall man to Sam. 'Put all your orders on hold.'

Sam looked around at his two customers. 'That won't take long,' he said.

'This is no time for jokes,' said the man wearing sunglasses. 'We work for The Firm. Has Matt Merton been in here today?'

'No,' said Sam. He wanted to protect his friend.

Matt was on the run from The Firm. He was hoping to hear from Jane, so he was staying close by. He had grabbed a coffee at the back door of Sam's cafe early that morning. Then he had disappeared.

'Don't lie to us, Sam,' said the man with sunglasses. He reached for his Truth Stick.

Sam was scared. They knew his name. What else did they know about him?

'What has Matt Merton told you about his work?' said the man with sunglasses.

'He never talks about his work,' Sam said. That was the truth. 'Can I get either of you a coffee?'

They did not answer him.

'You tell Matt Merton that we want to have a little talk with him,' said the tall man.

'Who will I say wants him?' asked Sam.

'Just tell him he had visitors,' they said. 'He'll know who we are.'

Sam did not say anything. The men glared at him. 'Do you understand what you have to do, Sam?'

Sam felt very scared. He stepped back.

The tall man jumped over the counter. He grabbed Sam and held him against the wall. 'If you forget to pass on the message, we will be back. We're watching you,' he said.

'And we'll make it "extra hot" for you if you lie to us,' smiled the man in sunglasses.

'With an extra shot too,' said the tall man, tapping the Truth Stick in his pocket.

They left Sam's cafe, knocking over a pile of coffee cups as they went.

Sam cleared up the mess. When he looked up, his two customers had gone.

CHAPTER 2

When Matt came into the cafe the next morning at dawn, Sam didn't look at him.

'Are you okay, Sam?' asked Matt.

'Go out the back door. The Firm were here,' said Sam. 'Run.'

Matt left and didn't look back.

Matt saw the fear in Sam's eyes. Matt didn't want to put Sam at risk. He had to get away fast.

Matt took the sky tram across the city. He kept looking behind him. The sky was grey and it was snowing again. Matt looked at his reflection in the window. 'Always winter, never summer,' he said to himself. 'How much time do I have left?'

Matt knew why there had been fear in Sam's eyes. Two men following him. Matt knew who they were. They came to The Firm when someone was in big trouble.

Matt got off the sky tram. He started to run, but they ran after him. Matt could not lose them.

He knew he had to do something clever to get rid of them.

Matt jumped on to the next sky tram. The two
men followed him. When the sky tram reached
its top speed, Matt forced open a door. He
jumped onto a sky tram going the other way.

But the men saw what he was doing and jumped with him. Matt forced the doors open again. He jumped onto another sky tram going back the other way. The men did the same.

'They are really good at this!' thought Matt, trying to get his breath back again. 'They've had better training than me. What can I do to get away from them?'

Suddenly Matt's phone bleeped. He had a text. Matt stopped. The two men stopped. They watched him as he read his message. They were waiting to see what his next move was going to be. This chase was a game to them. Matt read the text quickly.

Matt wanted to believe the message really was from Jane. The survival of the human race depended on it. He wanted to see her but he had to be sure it was not another trap. This time he would make sure it really was Jane.

Matt moved fast. He saw a car coming towards him and he flagged it down.

'I work for The Firm,' he said. 'Drive and don't look at my face.'

The driver did as he was told. There was fear in his eyes. Matt had lost the men for now but they would soon find him. There was no time to lose.

CHAPTER 3

Matt tried to work out a plan. What did Jane mean, 'The time is right'? Was she going to tell him why she ran off? Did she know what to do next?

Matt got out of the car and ran into the cafe in the park. A woman hiding her face behind a newspaper looked up. She smiled at him. It was Jane.

'Matt, I've missed you so much. I wanted to talk to you but it wasn't safe,' Jane said.

'Is it really you?' Matt asked.

Matt looked into her eyes. This time he knew it really was Jane. He squeezed her hand. He looked into her eyes and felt warm all over.

'Why wasn't it safe to see me?' said Matt. 'I've missed you so much. I tried so hard to find you.'

'Matt, it wasn't safe to see you because you worked for The Firm. You didn't remember anything from before The Crash. They drugged you. You didn't know you were killing humans. The Firm told you that you were killing The Enemy. You had become a slave to the aliens,' said Jane.

Matt could not look at her. Jane was right. It had taken him a long time to remember the truth. His mind was suddenly full of all the terrible things he had done. Full of all the people he had stopped on the street and killed.

Jane pulled his face round and made him look at her again. 'I've been watching you, Matt. I know you have changed. You know The Firm is evil. They will let the aliens take over the world unless we stop them. I know how to stop them. I need you to help me.'

Before they could talk about what to do, they heard shouting. The men were back.

'They're from The Firm. They've been chasing me all day. We have to get out of here,' said Matt.

Jane pulled at his arm. 'Follow me', she said. 'I know how we can get away.' She pulled him into the trees so they could hide. The two men passed them.

'This is my life,' she said. 'Always on the run.'

'Now it's mine too,' said Matt. 'We're in this together.'

Jane and Matt ran out of the park. They kept running until they reached Sam's cafe. Matt thought of the fear in Sam's eyes that morning. 'We can't put Sam in danger,' he said.

'Then tell him to get ready,' said Jane. 'We have to leave tonight. I'll come back for you.'

Matt pulled her close to him. It was time to say goodbye.

'Now that I've found you again Jane, I'll never let you go,' he said.

Jane smiled and looked up at him. 'I've got a plan, Matt. It's not going to be easy but we have to do it,' she said. 'We have to save the world.'

'I know,' said Matt. 'We'll be waiting. We'll do it together.'

He squeezed her hand. And they each ran into the shadows of the dark city, alone.

QUIZ

1. Who did the men in Sam's cafe work for?

2. What do they ask Sam?

3. What message did they give Sam for Matt?

4. How did they treat Sam?

5. How did Matt try to escape from the two agents?

6. Where did the text message tell Matt to go?

7. Why has Jane finally decided that it's safe to meet Matt?

8. What does Jane tell Matt about his work for the The Firm?

9. Why doesn't Matt hide in Sam's cafe?

10. When are Jane, Sam and Matt going to leave?

GLOSSARY

agent – someone who works for a company to provide a particular service

flagged down – stopped a car as it drove past

on hold – stop working on something

protect – prevent harm happening to someone or something

reflection – image bounced back from a shiny surface

ANSWERS

1. The Firm

2. Has Matt has been in the cafe that day? Does Matt ever talk about his work?

3. The agents want to speak to him

4. They threaten him

5. He jumped from one sky tram to another

6. The park

7. Because Matt knows The Firm is evil

8. He had killed humans and was a slave to the aliens

9. It would put Sam in danger

10. Tonight

CASE FILE

AUTHOR NAME
Paul Blum

JOB
Teacher

LAST KNOWN LOCATION
London, England

NOTES
Before The Crash taught in London schools.
Author of *The Extraordinary Files* and
Shadows. Believed to be in hiding from The
Firm. Wanted for questioning. Seems to know
more about the new ice age than he should ...

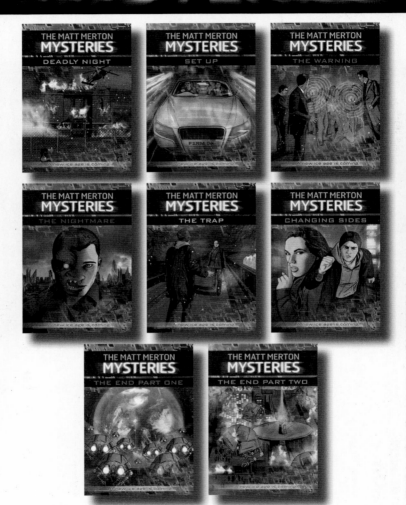